FAMILY LIFE:
Three brutal comedies

Wendy Hammond

357 W 20th St., NY NY 10011
212 627-1055

First printing: April 1990
ISBN: 0-88145-085-5

Book design: Marie Donovan
Word processing: WordMarc Composer Plus
Typographic controls: Xerox Ventura Publisher,
Professional Extension
Typeface: Palatino
Printed on acid-free paper and bound in the USA.

ABOUT THE AUTHOR

Wendy Hammond holds an MFA from NYU's Dramatic Writing Program, where she studied with Tina Howe, Len Jenkin, and Michael Weller. Jack Gelber directed her thesis play. Her play, THE GHOSTMAN, was first developed at the Sundance Institute, and then workshopped at the Long Wharf Theater, directed by John Tillinger. It will be produced by Charlotte Rep, the Salt Lake Acting Company, and the Stonehill Theater Project in New York City, all in 1990. Ms Hammond received a 1988 Drama League Award for her play JERSEY CITY, which will be produced off-Broadway by Second Stage in the 1989/1990 season. She received a 1989 McKnight Fellowship for Playwriting, and a 1989/90 grant for playwriting from the National Endowment for the Arts.

FAMILY LIFE originated in Bob Moss' workshop at
Playwrights Horizons. It was originally produced by
Home for Contemporary Theater and Art and the
Stonehill Theater Project, New York NY. It opened on
12 April 1989 with the following cast and creative
contributors:

THE TRANSMOGRIFICATION

JANE .... Paula Redinger
MRS WHITE .... Cecilia de Wolf
MR WHITE .... .Barry Kramer

MINNA AND THE SPACE PEOPLE

MINNA .... Sarah Halley
BRETT .... .Barry Kramer

MOM AND THE RAZOR BLADES

MOM .... Cecilia de Wolf
BETH .... Sarah Halley
ANNA .... Paula Redinger

Director .... .Barry Jay Kaplan
Set design .... .Geoffrey Makstutis
Costume design .... Donna Langman
Lighting design .... .Susi Levi
Sound design .... Andy Stein
Prop design .... Lou Storey
Stage manager .... Osiris Hertz
Production manager .... .Murphy Davis

CONTENTS

THE TRANSMOGRIFICATION

(A kitchen. MR WHITE sits at the table center, facing the audience, completely hidden behind the New York Post. *On his right sits MRS WHITE, on his left daughter JANE. The women watch him, trembling with terror, their forks poised above their untouched dinners. MR WHITE wears a black suit and bow tie with a white shirt. MR WHITE and JANE are also in black and white. The only color on stage is a giant pink bow in JANE's hair.)*

JANE

M-m-mom?

MRS WHITE

Sh.

(MR WHITE's hand appears from behind the the paper. He snaps his fingers then points to his empty plate. MRS WHITE jumps up, races to the counter, shovels more food on his plate, and runs back to the table. MR WHITE's hand grabs the plate and pulls it behind the paper. Horrible gobbling sounds. The plate reappears, empty.)

JANE

A-ask him.

MRS WHITE

Sssh.

(MR WHITE's hand snaps again and points to his martini glass. MRS WHITE jumps up, races to the counter, pours a

martini from a pitcher, throws in two olives, races back to the table. The martini glass disappears behind the paper. Horrible gurgling sounds. The martini glass reappears, empty.)

JANE

P-p-please?

MRS WHITE

In a minute.

(MR WHITE snaps and points to the martini glass, MRS WHITE races to fill it, MR WHITE's hand pulls it behind the paper, horrible gurgling sounds, and the glass reappears. JANE watches, trembling with terror, her fork poised over her dinner.)

MR WHITE

(From behind the paper) My boss called me a cockroach today.

MRS WHITE

Cockroach? *(Gets it)* Oh, it's a joke. Jane, it's a joke.

(Forced gales of laughter from MRS WHITE. JANE looks confused. Suddenly the paper smashes down on the table, giving us for the first time a view of MR WHITE's face, which is, at the moment, red and puffed with anger.)

MR WHITE

(Smashing the paper down) It's not FUNNY!

MRS WHITE

(Frantically) Of course not, dear. Not funny at—

MR WHITE

I work my GUTS out for that company. I come up with IDEAS! No one else around there has any ideas! I've got more ideas than all of 'em put together, but do they reward me?!

MRS WHITE

(Desperately) Not at all. They don't appreciate you one little—

MR WHITE

WRONG! THEY DO REWARD ME!

MRS WHITE

(Emphatically) They reward you. I was wrong—

MR WHITE

My boss says I'm a cockroach, THAT'S HOW THEY REWARD ME! He calls me into his office—he says I'm about as useful as an irritating BUG—he says he's tried to get rid of me but I just won't LEAVE—he called me a COCKROACH!

(MRS WHITE jumps up, hugs and strokes him.)

MRS WHITE

(Effusively) You're not a cockroach, I don't care what anybody says. The only reason he called you that is because he's jealous of you. Don't you think the man's jealous, Jane?

JANE

I th-th-th-th-ink m-maybe D-Daddy is b-bad at his j-j-j-j-job.

MR WHITE

(To MRS WHITE) When's she gonna learn how to talk? I can't understand a friggin' word.

MRS WHITE

We're working on it, dear.

JANE

A-ask him, M-m-mom.

MR WHITE

Where was I?

MRS WHITE

You were saying your boss is jealous of you.

MR WHITE

That's right. He's jealous. That's why he treats me like shit. I got ideas ten times better than his!

MRS WHITE

Of course you do. Of course.

MR WHITE

I know it. He knows it. He knows I know he knows it. He knows I know he knows everybody knows it. So he's jealous. I mean, who wouldn't be jealous?

MRS WHITE

Of course he's jealous. Of course.

MR WHITE

They're going to make me president of the company, you wait and see. Any day now. President of the whole damn company!

MRS WHITE

Any day. Any minute. Any second now that phone's going to ring. Don't you think so, Jane? Don't you think your father will make the best president the company ever had?

JANE

N-n-n-n-n-no since he d-doesn't seem to g-g-g-get along with p-p-people.

MR WHITE

(To MRS WHITE) You gotta do something with her. I can't understand a friggin' word.

JANE

P-p-please, Mom?

MRS WHITE

In a minute.

JANE

I'd ask him m-m-myself b-but he d-d-doesn't
understand a f-f-riggin word.

MR WHITE

Where was I?

MRS WHITE

President.

MR WHITE

President, that's right. I'm gonna be president of the
whole damn conglomerate. That's why my boss is
jealous of me.

MRS WHITE

Of course that's why. Of course.

MR WHITE

You know? I feel better. I think. I was depressed when I
came home from work, but now I think I feel better. I
think. Thank you, Snooks.

MRS WHITE

Anytime, Sweetums.

MR WHITE

(Pinching her cheeks) You are the cutest thing, Mufkie.

MRS WHITE

So are you. Pete.

JANE

M-m-mom?

MRS WHITE

All right, Jane.

JANE

P-p-please?

MRS WHITE

OK. Ah...Sugarlips?

MR WHITE

What?

MRS WHITE

We've got a....

MR WHITE

What?

MRS WHITE

We want to....Well....

MR WHITE

What.

MRS WHITE

Ah...well....

MR WHITE

What.

MRS WHITE

You see....

MR WHITE

WHAT.

MRS WHITE

It's just....

MR WHITE

WHAT!

JANE

W-w-w-we have s-s-s-s-something to ask
y-y-y-y-y-y-y-you.

MR WHITE

WHAT THE FUCK IS SHE SAYING?

MRS WHITE

We have something to ask you.

MR WHITE

(Calming down) Oh. OK. What.

MRS WHITE

Well. It'll mean so much to Jane.

MR WHITE

What!

MRS WHITE

Jane really has her heart set on it.

MR WHITE

WHAT.

MRS WHITE

I mean all day long she plays records—Beethoven,
Bach, Brahms—and she practices her dancing. So I
thought.... Well....

MR WHITE

WHAT!

MRS WHITE

In the middle of the night too. I get up to go to the
bathroom and there she is humming waltzes—Strauss
mostly—and dancing all around her room. So we were
wondering.... Well....

MR WHITE

WHAT!!! WHAT!!! WHAT!!!

MRS WHITE

I mean if you could see how lonely she looks as she
pirouettes across the back of the couch, tears streaming
down her face making puddles all over the cushions, so
we thought...ah....

MR WHITE

You're beginning to bug me.

MRS WHITE

Well...ah....

MR WHITE

You're really beginning to bug me.

MRS WHITE

We want....Well Jane wants....

MR WHITE

I am definitely BUGGED!

MRS WHITE

Well maybe Jane better tell you. Tell him, Jane.

JANE

I w-want to g-go to the ch-ch-church
d-d-d-d-d-d-d-d-d-d-d-d-d-d-d—

MRS WHITE

Come on, Jane.

JANE

d-d-d-d-d-d-d-d-d-d-d-d-d-d-d—

MRS WHITE

Come on!

JANE

d-d-dance tonight.

MR WHITE

WHAT THE FUCK IS SHE SAYING?

MRS WHITE

(Blurts) She wants to go to the church dance tonight.
(Winces)

(Silence)

MR WHITE

She what?

JANE

P-p-p-p-p-please?

MR WHITE

There's something I don't understand here. Who paid
for this house? Did you pay for this house?

MRS WHITE

No, dear.

MR WHITE

Did you pay for this house?

JANE

N-n-n-n-n-n-n-n—

MR WHITE

Then who paid for this house?

MRS WHITE:	JANE:
You did, dear.	Y-y-y-y-y-y-y—

MR WHITE

Who pays for food around here? Who pays for clothes and electricity and heat?

MRS WHITE:	JANE:
You do, dear.	Y-y-y-y-y-y-y—

MR WHITE

Who pays for TVs and VCRs and stereos and radios?

MRS WHITE:	JANE:
You do, dear.	Y-y-y-y-y-y-y—

MR WHITE

Who pays for refrigerators and washing machines and stoves and dishwashers and tables and chairs?

MRS WHITE:	JANE:
You do, dear.	Y-y-y-y-y-y-y—

MR WHITE

Who pays for sinks and counters and tiles and wallpaper and lamps and pans and dishes and silverware and glasses? Who pays for Ivory soap and Ajax cleanser and Mr. Clean?

MRS WHITE:	JANE:
You do, dear.	Y-y-y-y-y-y-y—

MR WHITE

And therefore, who is the boss around here? Who gets to make up the rules?

Mrs White:	Jane:
You do, dear.	Y-y-y-y-y-y-y—

MR WHITE

Good. Very good. Now I seem to recall a rule, one of the most important rules, that says that my daughter and my wife are supposed to be here each evening when I get home from working my GUTS out ALL DAY. That they are supposed to take CARE of me, give me LOVE and AFFECTION. They are NOT supposed to ABANDON me. They are NOT supposed to FORSAKE me for things like church dances after I've been DEFILED and DEBASED and ABUSED and HUMILIATED ALL DAY EVERY DAY AT WORK so that they can have things like TVs and VCRs and stereos and radios and refrigerators and washing machines and stoves and dishwashers and tables and chairs and sinks and counters and tiles and wallpaper and lamps and pans and dishes and silverware and glasses and Ivory soap and Ajax cleanser and Mr. CLEAN!

JANE

M-m-m-mom? Help m-m-m-m-me.

MR WHITE

Can't you shut her UP!

JANE

I w-w-w-w-w-want to g-go to the d-d-d-d-d-d-ance.

MRS WHITE

(Terrified) Ah...well...it's just we've been thinking, dear. Jane isn't so young anymore. Most girls her age have careers and families by now. What's so awful about letting her go out just this once?

MR WHITE

Wait a minute. You're defying me.

MRS WHITE

No. I'm just...asking a question. I think I should
be...allowed to ask a question...now and then.... And I
think Jane...should be allowed to go to this dance!

MR WHITE

My God. This is mutiny.

MRS WHITE

If that's how you want to put it.

(Pause)

MR WHITE

I seem to recall there was once another mutiny. Do you
remember that mutiny?

MRS WHITE

Yes.

MR WHITE

What happened after that mutiny?

MRS WHITE

You put us out. You locked the doors.

MR WHITE

And?

MRS WHITE

It was cold.

MR WHITE

And?

MRS WHITE

We got frostbite.

MR WHITE

And?

MRS WHITE

Jane lost a finger and I lost three toes.

MR WHITE

Good. Very good. Now I am going to read my paper
and there will be no more talk of mutiny. Terrible
things happen when there is talk of mutiny. Betrayers
are punished. Remember Brutus? Remember Judas?

*(He opens the paper, completely covering himself again. His
hand appears from behind the paper, snaps and points to his
empty plate. MRS WHITE jumps up, shovels more food on the
plate, and throws it back on the table. MR WHITE pulls it
behind the paper. Horrible gobbling sounds. Immediately the
plate appears, empty.)*

JANE

(To MR WHITE) I d-d-d-don't have any f-f-friends.

MRS WHITE

Sssh.

JANE

I w-want g-g-g-go to the d-dance so I c-can make
friends.

MRS WHITE

(Whispers) Let him read, Sweetheart. He's had a bad
day.

JANE

(To MR WHITE) Other p-p-p-p-p-people have friends.

MRS WHITE

Sssh.

JANE

W-w-w-why can't I?

MRS WHITE

We'll ask him tomorrow.

JANE

(*To* MRS WHITE) Ask him n-now! I'm t-tired of
tomorrow. I am th-thirty-five-years old and I've never
made any friends. I want to go to the dance tonight!

MRS WHITE

Jane, your stutter!

JANE

I want to go to the dance!

MRS WHITE

Your stutter is gone!

JANE

(*Joyously*) Please let me go to the dance!

MRS WHITE

(*Joyously*) Please let Jane go to the dance, please!

(MR WHITE *slams down the paper. Silence.*)

MR WHITE

(*Very calmly*) You know? You are really really bugging
me. In fact, you're beginning to look like a bug. In fact,
you're beginning to look like a cockroach.

MRS WHITE

Cockroach?

MR WHITE

Yes.

MRS WHITE
(Gets it) Oh, it's a joke. Jane, it's a joke.

(Forced gales of laughter from MRS WHITE.*)*

MR WHITE
IT'S NOT FUNNY! *(Immediately she is silent.)* What's that?

MRS WHITE
What?

MR WHITE
On your arm.

MRS WHITE
Where?

MR WHITE
There.

MRS WHITE
I don't see anything.

MR WHITE
I do. It's changing color.

MRS WHITE
(Brush off) No.

MR WHITE
Cockroach color.

MRS WHITE
I don't think so

MR WHITE
Oh my God.

MRS WHITE

What?

MR WHITE

Your eyes are getting bigger.

MRS WHITE

Oh now....

MR WHITE

You're growing antenna. Little insect legs are popping
out of your body—

MRS WHITE

Don't be silly—

MR WHITE

You're doubting my word?

MRS WHITE

No, but—

MR WHITE

I've always been right before.

MRS WHITE

I know, but—

MR WHITE

I'm boss in this house. Right?

MRS WHITE

Yes, you're the boss, but—

MR WHITE

Jane? Isn't she looking more and more like a cockroach?
(*Standing over* JANE) Tell the truth.

                          JANE
W-w-well. Sh-sh-she is ch-ch-changing c-c-c-colors.

                       MR WHITE
She is changing colors.

                      MRS WHITE
I thought you couldn't understand a word Jane says.

                       MR WHITE
You thought wrong. (To JANE—pointing to MRS WHITE's
head) What are those up there, Jane?

                          JANE
Ant-t-tenna.

                       MR WHITE
See?

                      MRS WHITE
I can't change into a cockroach just because you say so.

                       MR WHITE
Oh no? Look at that.

(He holds a shiny pan in front of her face. She looks into the
reflection and screams.)

                      MRS WHITE
OH MY GOD! OH MY GOD! (She starts running around
in circles, trying to pull the skin off her arms and face.)
HELP! HELP! WHAT DO I DO! WHAT DO I DO!

                       MR WHITE
I'M not the cockroach. My boss was wrong. YOU'RE
the fucking cockroach. It's YOU.

                          JANE
(Anguished) M-m-m-m-m-m-m-m-m-m-mom!

(MRS WHITE *screams and doubles over.*)

MRS WHITE

MY BODY IS CHANGING! I CAN FEEL IT! MY BODY
IS CHANGING!

(MRS WHITE'S *body curls and writhes as it changes into the
shape of a cockroach.*)

JANE

D-d-don't l-l-l-listen to him!

MR WHITE

(*As* MRS WHITE *changes*) It's finally coming out, how
disgusting you are—how ugly YOU REALLY
FUCKING ARE.

JANE

D-don't let him d-d-d-do this!

MR WHITE

The way you grovel before me, it's fucking
DISGUSTING. The way you try to please me doing
every little thing I say—

JANE

D-d-on't b-believe him!

MR WHITE

Tonight's the second time in your life you ever even
QUESTIONED me and look where it's got you.
YOU'RE TURNING INTO A COCKROACH!

JANE

He's n-not God, he's just y-your husband! D-d-don't
b-believe him!

MR WHITE

You HAVE to believe me, you disgusting little
cockroach, you can't think for yourself. Every thought
in your head was put there by ME. You're not a person
you're a BLOB, a little fucking spineless BUG, scurrying
around every time I fucking snap my fingers!

JANE

Ty-tyrant!

MR WHITE

I fucking HATE being married to you, do you fucking
know that? Whimpering, simpering — this whole
fucking marriage — you've fucking disGUSTED me
and now I fucking know why.

JANE

D-d-dictator!

MR WHITE

You're a fucking COCKROACH! That's why my
fucking boss fucking called me that today. Your fucking
cockroachness fucking rubbed the fuck on ME!

MRS WHITE

Help me! Please! I don't want to be a cockroach!

MR WHITE

Then you better choose. Either you're MY WIFE. Or
you're her mother THE COCKROACH.

JANE

D-d-don't l-l-listen to h-h-him!

MRS WHITE

NOOOOOOOOOOOOOOOOOOOOOOOOOO! *(Silence)* I'm
not the cockroach! I'M NOT THE COCKROACH! *(She*

points a twisted finger at JANE.) SHE'S THE
COCKROACH!

>   JANE

C-c-c-c-c-cockroach? *(Gets it)* Oh, it's a j-j-j-j-joke.
R-right? *(Gales of forced laughter)*

>   MRS WHITE

IT'S NOT FUNNY!

(Immediately JANE *is quiet.* MRS WHITE's *body begins
straightening out.)*

>   MR WHITE

(Pointing to JANE*)* What's that?

>   MRS WHITE

(Taking the cue) Yeah. What's that?

>   JANE

W-w-w-what?

>   MRS WHITE

Your arms are changing color.

>   JANE

(Brush off) N-n-n-n-n-n-no.

>   MR WHITE

She's calling you a liar.

>   MRS WHITE

ARE YOU CALLING YOUR MOTHER A LIAR?

>   JANE

N-no—

>   MRS WHITE

Good. Because mothers don't lie. Do they?

JANE

N-n-n-n-n-n-n-n-n-n-n-n-n—

MRS WHITE

DO THEY?!

JANE

M-m-m-m-mothers d-d-don't l-l-l-lie.

MRS WHITE

If I say your arms are changing color, THEY'RE
CHANGING COLOR!

MR WHITE

Good. Very good.

MRS WHITE

Look! Your eyes are getting big. (MRS WHITE *has now
resumed her human shape.*)

JANE

D-d-d-daddy, is it t-true?

MRS WHITE

OF COURSE IT'S TRUE. MOTHER SAYS SO. Look!
Little insect legs are popping out all over your body!

JANE

Oh n-no! (JANE *doubles over. She begins to twist and writhe
into the shape of a cockroach.*) D-d-don't d-d-d-do this,
M-mom! P-please!

MRS WHITE

I never wanted a child, did you know that? I HATE
children! I HATE THEM. They're DISGUSTING.

MR WHITE

Fucking disgusting.

MRS WHITE

They're FUCKING disgusting. Crying and puking and pissing and shitting and getting their periods! CAN YOU IMAGINE ANYTHING MORE FUCKING DISGUSTING?

JANE

(As she changes) P-p-please d-don't do this to m-me!

MRS WHITE

And now you're fucking turning into a fucking cockroach which is even MORE FUCKING DISGUSTING!

JANE

S-stop it! M-m-m-m-m-mom!

MRS WHITE

That's why your father fucking called ME a fucking cockroach. YOUR fucking cockroachness fucking rubbed the fuck on ME!

JANE

(Writhing) P-p-p-p-p-lease ! P-p-p-p-p-leeeeeeeeeeeee.... *(*JANE *is now on the floor, completely in the shape of a cockroach. High-pitched insect squeaking noises come from her mouth.)*

MR WHITE

Pretty good. For a woman.

MRS WHITE

Thanks.

MR WHITE

I think we better call the exterminator.

MRS WHITE

Oh no. For one little bug?

MR WHITE

A pretty big bug.

MRS WHITE

I think it's cold, poor thing. Maybe I better go get it a blanket.

MR WHITE

Bugs don't need blankets. Bugs need exterminators. Snuggums. *(He kisses her.)*

MRS WHITE

I'll call 'em first thing in the morning. Snuckie.

MR WHITE

(Pinching her cheeks) You are the cutest thing.

MRS WHITE

You're pretty cute yourself, Pumpkin Buns.

(They kiss. She pulls away.)

MRS WHITE

I don't know, Silky Tums. I feel...well....Did I really have to turn Jane into a....

MR WHITE

Can't be helped now, my little Pie Face. It's done.

MRS WHITE

I guess so.

MR WHITE

How 'bout let's go to bed, Sugarlips.

MRS WHITE

Good idea, Fancy Fingers.

(They start to exit, arm in arm.)

MR WHITE
You know something, Snooks?

MRS WHITE
What, Tingle Tongue?

MR WHITE
I was depressed when I came home from work, you
know? But now I feel so much better.

(They exit. JANE *is left behind on the floor in the shape of a
cockroach, making high-pitched insect squeaking noises.)*

LIGHTS FADE OUT

MINNA AND THE SPACE PEOPLE

(MINNA—*in an old Woolworth's housedress, her hands in fists—stands facing* BRETT. BRETT—*in a rumpled business suit, his lips pursed—stands facing* MINNA. *Throughout the scene he pops pills and then candy into his mouth, arranges items on the table into geometric configurations, and dabs his brow with a handkerchief which he then folds carefully into a tiny little square. Overlapping:*)

MINNA
YOU WILL NOT KILL MY BABY!

BRETT
It's not killing. It's taking it out of your body for awhile.

MINNA
YOU HAVE NO RIGHT KILLING MY BABY!

BRETT
They'll take it away from you! They don't let babies stay in the nuthouse!

MINNA
YOU WON'T KILL MY BABY! I WON'T LET YOU KILL MY BABY!

BRETT
I'm not killing it, THE DOCTOR IS KILLING IT! I didn't mean that. Minna, you are driving me CRAZY!

MINNA

(Pointing to her stomach) This baby is more important
than Jesus Christ.

BRETT

Minna, they don't let lunatics raise children in the loony
bin.

MINNA

This baby will save the world from nuclear holocaust.

BRETT

Is that what you want, Minna? You want them to give
your baby away?

MINNA

Jesus Christ didn't save the world from nuclear
holocaust. Jesus Christ just said to turn the other cheek!

BRETT

You want maniacs getting ahold of it? You want the
Steinbergs raising your child?

MINNA

They WON'T be raising it, that's what I'm trying to tell
you. You could call a sanity hearing. You could say
Mom and Dad made a mistake, I'm really NOT crazy.
You're my brother. You could tell them I never once did
anything crazy the whole time we were growing up.

BRETT

Minna—

MINNA

I never did anything crazy, right?

BRETT

This isn't the—

MINNA

The whole time we were growing up. Never once!

BRETT

We're off the subject.

MINNA

This IS the subject. I never did anything crazy, right?

BRETT

The subject is you've got to have an abortion.

MINNA

I'm not talking to you 'til you tell me I'm right. I never did anything crazy.

BRETT

Minna! (MINNA *sits on the floor, closes her eyes, and puts her fingers in her ears.*) All right. You're right.

MINNA

About what?

BRETT

You're right about not being crazy when we were growing up.

MINNA

(*Jumping up*) That's right. So all you have to do is tell them that at the hearing and then buy me a little apartment and a little crib and some food—

BRETT

I can't buy you an apartment—

MINNA

Yes you CAN!

BRETT

I don't have the money.

MINNA

Yes you DO!

BRETT

No I DON'T!

MINNA

YOU AND RITA MAKE LOTS OF MONEY!

BRETT

WE ALSO HAVE LOTS OF BILLS!

MINNA

CUT BACK!

BRETT

WE CAN'T!

MINNA

YES YOU CAN!

BRETT

NO WE CAN'T!

MINNA

YES YOU CAN!

BRETT

NO WE CAN'T! NO WE CAN'T! NO WE CAN'T!

(MINNA *stomps her foot, then plops down furiously into a chair facing away from* BRETT. *Then* BRETT *stomps his foot and plops down furiously into a chair facing away from* MINNA.)

BRETT

OK. Who's the father? Maybe I could figure this out better if you told me who the father is.

MINNA

There isn't a father.

BRETT

There has to be a—

MINNA

The space people put her inside me.

BRETT

Space people. *(Dabs brow and pops pills)*

MINNA

They took me into their spaceship and put a machine on my stomach and told me I would now bear a girl child who would save the world from nuclear holocaust.

BRETT

How did you get into their ship?

MINNA

They came to me at night—they're really weird looking, I was scared out of my mind—and they made me stand this certain way. Then all of a sudden I was out of the hospital and zooming straight up in the air.

BRETT

Minna, there has to be a father. I was sitting right next to you when Mom explained the facts of life to us, so I know you know there has to be a father.

MINNA

Jesus Christ didn't have a father.

BRETT

Then who did you have sex with? You had to have sex
with SOMEbody!

MINNA

The space people told me not to have sex.

BRETT

Stop talking about the space people! There's no such
thing as space people!

MINNA

Then how come I talk to them all the time? How come
they tell me how to be happy? How come they want to
talk to you and tell you how to be happy too?

BRETT

(Pops pills and candy) I am happy.

MINNA

You fight with Rita all the time.

BRETT

I do not.

MINNA

Rita drinks so much you have to call her work and
make excuses. Sometimes she hits you just like Mom
did.

BRETT

(Flaring) She doesn't—!

MINNA

Sometimes she throws things at you.

BRETT

(Collects himself) Rita drinks no more than anyone else
and she never hits me.

MINNA

Then how come you have a giant bruise on your back?

BRETT

I don't have a bruise on my back.

MINNA

Yes.

BRETT

No!

MINNA

The space people told me. You were fighting. You turned away. She threw the vacuum cleaner at your back.

BRETT

We're off the subject again! The subject is you having an abortion!

MINNA

(Jumping up) I WILL NOT HAVE AN ABORTION!

BRETT

(Jumping up) YOU DON'T HAVE A CHOICE!

MINNA

YOU HAVE A CHOICE! YOU CAN SAVE MY BABY!

BRETT

I CAN'T SAVE YOUR BABY!

MINNA

ALL YOU HAVE TO DO IS GET ME OUT OF HERE AND GIVE ME A LITTLE MONEY!

BRETT

I DON'T HAVE A LITTLE MONEY!

MINNA

THEN GET ME OUT OF HERE AND I'LL FIND THE
MONEY!

BRETT

I CAN'T GET YOU OUT OF HERE! YOU'RE NOT
READY TO GET OUT OF HERE!

MINNA

YES I AM!

BRETT

NO YOU'RE NOT!

MINNA

SAYS WHO?

BRETT

SAYS YOUR DOCTORS!

MINNA

WHAT DO THEY KNOW?

BRETT

THEY KNOW YOU'RE CRAZY!

MINNA

I AM NOT CRAZY!!!

BRETT

YOU BELIEVE IN SPACE PEOPLE! THAT'S CRAZY!!!!

MINNA

(Deep breath) You mean you're not going to help me?

BRETT

No.

MINNA

You won't help save the savior of the world?

BRETT

No.

MINNA

What if Jesus had been an abortion? Think of that.

BRETT

Jesus' mother didn't live in a nuthouse.

(Beside herself, MINNA kicks a chair, then plops down into it, facing away from BRETT.)

BRETT

Minna, someday, if you do everything the doctors tell you, maybe you'll get out of here. And then you'll find a job and a husband and then you can start a family, a normal family. Isn't that what you really want? Isn't that the way you really really want it? *(MINNA doesn't respond.)* Minna, come on. Talk to me, OK? *(MINNA doesn't respond.)* I just think it'll be easier to have this abortion now than to give the baby away later. *(MINNA doesn't respond.)* You know I'm right. I know you know I'm right. *(MINNA doesn't respond.)* Minna, we gotta talk about this. We're not going to get anywhere if we don't start talking. *(MINNA doesn't respond. BRETT picks up the Christmas present and drops it in MINNA's lap.)* The least you could do is open your Christmas present.

(MINNA rips the bow and paper off, opens the box, and pulls out a scarf and a glass fish. She reaches into her bra and takes out a lighter.)

BRETT

Where did you get that? You're not supposed to have that! *(MINNA sets the scarf on fire.)* MINNA!

(BRETT *lunges for the scarf, throws it on the ground, and stomps the fire out. Meanwhile* MINNA *has picked up the fish and calmly placed it on the floor. She stomps on the fish, smashing it into tiny pieces of glass.*)

BRETT

MINNA MINNA! STOP IT STOP IT! (*But the glass fish is destroyed.* BRETT *crosses to the glass bits and begins picking them up.* MINNA *stands, watching him.* BRETT *is blinking back tears.*) I spent three lunch hours shopping for this. Three! I could have been clearing my desk. I could have been making phone calls or seeing clients or dictating reports, but no, I was searching and searching for the exact perfect replica of the little glass fish you had when we were kids. And now you've smashed it to bits. Three hours wasted. I work 'til nine every night, do you have any idea what that's like? I get home at ten, eat, do the dishes, take the garbage out, go to bed, then get up at 5:30 the next morning and start the whole thing again! I ask Rita to help with the garbage but...well, things can get tense in a marriage....And now you want to have a baby and I don't care WHAT you say I just know I'M the one who's going to end up taking care of you AND your baby and Rita's not going to like that at ALL, not at ALL! And when Rita doesn't like things...well I don't want to talk about Rita. Don't move. You'll cut yourself.

MINNA

What do you care?

BRETT

You think I don't care?

MINNA

The only reason you're here is because Nurse Doyle called you and said you better make me get an abortion quick.

BRETT

That isn't the only reason.

MINNA

You never visited me before.

BRETT

I call you all the time but you always hang up on me.
Why do you always hang up on me?

MINNA

Why didn't you stop Mom and Dad from putting me in
here?

BRETT

How? I wasn't around.

MINNA

No. You ran away and left me there.

BRETT

I had to run away. You know I had to.

MINNA

You could've taken me with you.

BRETT

You were too young.

MINNA

Yeah. Well they were worse after you left. I got all of it.
And then Dwayne got me pregnant but Mom made me
have the baby. I had to drop out of school, I had to give
the baby away, and then I started having these temper
problems and I couldn't stop yelling at people and once
I threw eggs at the front door and the windows—I
broke some of the windows—so Mom brought me here
and told them I was crazy.

> BRETT

Jesus, Minna. I didn't know all that.

> MINNA

You could have found out.

> BRETT

Didn't you tell the doctors what happened?

> MINNA

I couldn't stop crying long enough to talk. No matter
what drug they gave me, no matter how hard I tried, I
couldn't stop crying.

> BRETT

You're not crying now.

> MINNA

Not for years. Not since the space people taught me
how to be happy. They've even given me a baby again.
(MINNA *reaches under her dress and pulls out a mascara
wand hidden in her underwear. She unscrews the wand, talks
into one end and listens to the other.*) Yes? Now? (*To*
BRETT) They want to talk to you.

> BRETT

The space people?

> MINNA

Yeah.

> BRETT

(*Upset*) Minna.

> MINNA

(*Talking into the wand*) I don't think he's in the
mood....OK....Will he give it back?...If you say so.... (*To*
BRETT) I'm supposed to take a nap now—they say the
baby needs it. And I'm supposed to leave this here so

you can talk to them in private. Drop it off in my room
when you're done. Oh yeah. They say they've figured
out how you can earn a lot more money so you can
support me and the baby. (MINNA *sets the mascara wand
on the table in front of* BRETT *and exits, humming a
Christmas carol.*)

BRETT
(Calling after her) Minna! If you think I'm going to talk
into this thing you're out of your mind!

(But she's gone. BRETT *gathers up his briefcase and coat,
starts to leave, but then stops. He looks at the mascara wand.
He picks it up, looks it over, then raises it to his ear and
listens. His eyes widen.)*

BRETT
(Into the mascara wand) Yeah?... Yeah?...

LIGHTS FADE

MOM AND THE RAZOR BLADES

(Author's note: The props in this play can be unrealistic, such as two-dimensional cartoon drawings. ANNA can be played by a man in a little girl skirt, until he comes out at the end with the suitcase, when he's wearing pants.)

(Lights up on the living room: a couch, mirror, ironing table, music stand, violin, guitar, trash can, a table with a birthday cake on it, and several cleaning items. Center stage is a door soon to be known as Father's Office.)

(MOM runs on, wearing heels, stockings, and a full body girdle. She places a dress on the ironing table and irons it. Her hair is much like Jackie Kennedy's was in the mid 1960's.)

MOM
(As she irons) Beth? Anna? Don't you want to come help your mother? *(No answer)* Brett? Spencer? *(No answer)* Clifford? *(No answer)* It's your mother's birthday. Bobbie? Doesn't anyone want to help their mother on her birthday? *(She puts on her dress in front of the mirror.)* Isn't anyone going to help their mother clean for her own birthday party? *(No answer)* Jimmy? Jerry? Johnnie? Jody? Jamie? Josie? Jenny? Jannie? Joshie? Jeremy? Janie? Jerry? Joey? George? *(No answer)* Julie? Jeffery? *(Whimpers)* Tad? *(No answer)* It's awful quiet around here. Are you planning a birthday surprise? Are my children planning a birthday surprise for their mother?

(BETH, eleven years old, enters crawling; a pad of paper and pen hang from a string around her neck. She crawls to the middle of the floor and begins writing furiously. BETH doesn't walk, but crawls, until otherwise instructed. She is played by an adult.)

MOM

(Panicked) Get up! Get up! Your father's coming out of his office any minute! Your father's coming out of his office any minute! What if he trips over you! What if he trips over you!

(BETH rips a page off her pad and drops it on the floor, then continues writing furiously on the next page.)

MOM

(Pointing to the page on the floor) No! No! Bad girl! We don't made MESSES! You know how your father feels about MESSES! Pick it up. *(BETH doesn't.)* Pick it UP! *(BETH doesn't. MOM reaches under the couch and pulls out a mean-looking wooden baseball bat. She hold the bat over BETH's head.)* PICK IT UP! *(BETH picks up the paper.)* Good. Now I want you to put this note under the door for your father. *(Takes a note out of her pocket and reads)* "Dearest husband. If it's not too much trouble, could you please come to my birthday party? Your loving wife." Well I think that should do it. *(BETH scribbles a note and hands it to MOM. She reads.)* "He's not going to come." You never know, Beth. He might. I think it pays to always think the best of people. *(BETH scribbles another note and hands it to MOM. She reads.)* "He hasn't come out of his office in 25 years." He had to figure out the phone bill, Beth. Phone bills sometimes take awhile to figure out. Now put this under the door!!! *(Trembling with fear, BETH makes her way to the door and slides the note under the office door. Immediately a note slides back out. Mom picks it up and reads.)* "I'm sick of your notes, Doris. One more note and I'll have to do something drastic."

Oh dear. *(Blinks back tears)* Well I'm sure he wouldn't
mind notes from the children. Beth, will you write a
note to your father and ask him to come to my birthday
party? *(*BETH *writes a note and hands it to* MOM. MOM
reads.) "I can't." Good heavens. Why not? *(*BETH *writes
another note.)* "I'm scared." What are you scared of,
Beth? *(*BETH *writes another note.)* "I've never met the
man. Who knows what he's like." What does it matter
what he's like, Beth. He's your father. *(*BETH *crawls
under the table.)* All right. I'll write one for you. *(*MOM
writes—) "Dearest Dad. Please come to Mom's birthday
party. Signed Beth." I'll have to get the bat, Beth
sweetie, unless you PUT THIS UNDER THE DOOR.
(Trembling, BETH *slides the note under the door.* MOM
*waits, tingling with excitement. No note returns. Instead, a
scraping noise starts.)* Did you hear that, Beth? He's
moving around! I think he's coming out! *(*MOM *quickly
fixes her hair then poses, ready to greet him. But the door
doesn't open. She is devastated.)* Maybe he recognizes it's
my handwriting. Beth? Please write him a note, please?
All you have to say is "Daddy, when you coming out?"
*(*BETH *writes one word on a page, rips the page off, and
throws it on the floor.)* No! No! Bad girl! *(*BETH *continues
writing one word on a page and throwing pages on the floor.)*
You want me to get the baseball bat? *(*BETH *continues
throwing pages on the floor.)* Oh well. *(*MOM *picks up a
page, runs across the room, and throws it in the trash can.)* I
guess I don't have the heart to discipline you kids. I just
let you run wild. Wild! *(She runs back to* BETH, *picks
another page off the floor, and runs to the trash can.* BETH
continues throwing pages on the floor and MOM *continues
running back and forth from* BETH *to the trash can until
otherwise instructed. As she runs,* MOM *says loudly to the
door.)* If your father came out of his office we'd have
some discipline around here. If your father came out of
his office he'd put some order in the house.

(ANNA, *ten years old, enters, carrying an enormous stack of* *books.* ANNA *is also played by an adult.*)

ANNA
(Urgently) Mom! I gotta talk to you!

MOM
(Still running back and forth) What about, dear?

ANNA
I think there's something wrong with the family!

MOM
(Still running) There's nothing wrong with our family. We have a lovely, lovely family. We're well educated, upper-middle class. We believe in God and Jesus Christ. We go to church four times a week—

ANNA
You don't go to church. Dad hasn't let you out of the house for 1463 days.

MOM
(Still running) Well, I would go to church if I could. We have 37 beautiful children, a brilliant, successful father, and a mother who loves you so much, so very much, so so so very very much, so so so so so so so so so so so so so so so very very much much much much much much much much much much—

ANNA
I know you love us! Mom, would you please sit down and listen to me?

MOM
(Running faster and faster) I can't sit down. I have to clean this place for my birthday party. This house is never clean. I clean and clean but it never gets clean. I

never get to rest. There is no rest for the wicked the
Bible says. I must be so wicked. So very wicked. So so
so very very wicked. So so so so so so so so so so so
very very wicked wicked wicked wicked—

ANNA
Beth! (BETH *looks up.*) Stop it, OK? (BETH *stops writing
and throwing papers on the floor.* MOM *collapses on the
couch, exhausted.*)

ANNA
There's something wrong, Mom. Brett and Spencer are
heroin addicts. Robin, Robbie, and Bob are in jail.
Mary's a mass murderer. Randy's a rapist. Thad is a
thief. Candy sells crack and Sandy snorts coke. And the
rest of the kids have either flunked out of or been
kicked out of school.

MOM
Sandy does not snort coke.

ANNA
See for yourself. (*She holds up objects on the table.*) Mirror.
Razor blades. Cocaine. Now, according to the family
therapy books I've been reading (*Checks her notes*) these
are all symptoms of deeply rooted family problems.
(*Sounds of scraping noises coming from Father's Office*)

MOM
Anna, do you hear that noise? I wonder what he's
doing in there.

ANNA
Mom, you gotta listen to me!

MOM

They're just going through a phase, dear. When you're
a mother you'll understand that children are always
going through phases.

ANNA

What about Henry, David, Scott, Cindy, and Pat?

MOM

What about them?

ANNA

They all committed suicide. Suicide's a phase one can
never grow out of.

MOM

(Weeping) Oh the grief! The grief! (Overcome with sobs) I
keep asking myself why? Why did they do it? They had
everything. Money. Education. A brilliant, successful
father and a mother who loved them so much, so very
much, so so so very very much, so so so so so so so so
so so so so so so so very very much much much much
much much much much much much—

ANNA

I know you loved them!

MOM

I don't think you do. I don't think children really
understand about love. They haven't the capacity.
(MOM gestures and accidently slaps BETH.) It takes being a
mother to really learn about—

ANNA

Mom! Look at Beth! (BETH is slapping herself.) That's
what Joey was doing last night before he hung himself!

MOM

Oh no! Not Joey too! *(Heartwrenching sobs)*

ANNA

We gotta do something fast before the whole family is killed!

MOM

But what can we do?

ANNA

Therapy.

MOM

(Panicked) Therapy?

ANNA

(Checking her notes) Jungian, Freudian, Reichian, Adlerian, Lowian, Piagetian, Masserian, Frankian, Millerian, Horneyian, Laingian, Rogerian, Jonesian, Johnsonian, Gestalt, Transactional, Peckian, Ericksonian as in Milton and Eriksonian as in Erik! We'll do them all if that's what it takes!

MOM

Beth! You're not wearing shoes! You'll get grease spots on the carpet! Go put your shoes on this minute!

(BETH is now writing furiously. She ignores MOM.)

ANNA

First individual and then family therapy.

MOM

(To BETH) THIS MINUTE!!

ANNA
We'll start with you, Mom, since according to my
family therapy books "the parents are responsible for
behavioral dynamics within the family."

MOM
But why would I need therapy? I have my faults, I
know, but I am certainly not CRAZY. BETH PUT
YOUR SHOES ON THIS MINUTE OR I'LL GET THE
BAT!!!

ANNA
She doesn't wear shoes, Mom. She doesn't walk.

MOM
If you don't put your shoes on right now you'll get
cancer. I read about this in *Better Homes and Gardens*.
Going barefoot on carpet causes cancer of the feet.
(Pointing to BETH's *feet)* LOOK! IT'S STARTING
ALREADY!!!!

(Terrified, BETH *crawls quickly off.)*

ANNA
(Picking up BETH's *writing pad)* Mom, listen to this.
"Dark knives stabbing—black blood warm in my eye
sockets—intestines slide across red-slimed floors."

MOM
I don't think writing should depress people, do you? I
think writing should cheer people up.

ANNA
But Mom. You don't understand. Johnnie was writing
stuff like this yesterday before he threw himself under a
car.

MOM
(Weeping) Oh no! Not Johnnie too!

ANNA

And it looks like Beth is next! Mom, we gotta do
therapy fast!

MOM

But can't I have my birthday party? I promise I'll do
anything to keep my children alive. But first may I
please have my birthday party? (BETH *crawls in, wearing
socks. She holds her feet up to show* MOM, *but* MOM *doesn't
notice.*) It's the one day of the year when the party's for
ME. When I get appreciated. When I'm not cleaning or
cooking or comforting or changing diapers or weeding
the lawn or going without food so my children can eat
or going without clothes so I can keep my children
warm or going without sleep staying up all night
washing orange crayon scribbles off the wall.

(BETH *is now trying to choke herself.*)

ANNA

Beth! Stop! (*Runs to her*)

MOM

For a few moments each year my family sings to ME,
gives ME presents, tells ME they love ME so much, so
very much, so so so very very much, so so so so so so so
so so so so so so so so so very very much much much
much much much much much much much—

ANNA

Mom, we'll have a birthday party! (ANNA *has finally
succeeded in getting* BETH's *hands away from her throat.*)
Beth, do you think you can keep from killing yourself
long enough for a birthday party? (BETH *writes
furiously.*) OK, Mom. We'll try it. But if Beth starts
displaying suicidal tendencies again, we'll have to stop.

MOM

Good. *(Calling)* Brett? Spencer? Clifford? It's time for
my birthday party! *(To* ANNA*)* Why don't they answer?
(To Father's Office door) Sweetheart? It's time to come
out! It's time for my birthday party! *(No answer)* Jimmy?
Jerry? Jody? Johnnie? Jamie? Josie? Jenny? Jannie?
Joshie? Jeremy? Janie? Jerry? Joey? George? *(No answer)*
Julie? Jeffery? *(No answer)* Tad? *(Excited)* It's awful quiet
around here. I wonder why it's so quiet? Do you think
it's a birthday surprise? *(*BETH *hands* MOM *an envelope.*
MOM *smiles with delight and opens it. Reading.)* "If you
think it's a little quiet around here—" *(Smiles, excited,
turns the page)* "that's because we've run away, all of us
except Beth and Anna. Oh yeah. Jimmie didn't run
away either. He stuck his head in the lawn mower so he
couldn't." *(Weeping)* Oh no! Not Jimmie too!

ANNA

Mom. I'm sorry.

MOM

Thirty-five children either dead or gone!

ANNA

I'm really sorry.

MOM

What about you? Are you going to run away too?

ANNA

'Course not, Mom.

MOM

Why not? It seems to be the going thing around here. I
must be a terrible mother!

ANNA

You're a good mother, Mom.

MOM

I must be terrible. Why else would thirty-five children
either kill themselves or run away?

ANNA

I don't know. But all the psychologists agree, it's not the
mother's fault. We're all just victims of victims.

MOM

Is that what you think?

ANNA

Yes I do.

MOM

Then you don't hate me for failing you in some terrible
way?

ANNA

No Mom. I love you very much.

MOM

You do?

ANNA

So much. So very much.

MOM

So so so very very much? So so so so so so so so so—

ANNA

All that!

MOM

Oh thank you. Thank you for being my beautiful
daughter. (Embraces ANNA. There is the sound of scraping
from Father's Office.) There's that noise again. I wonder
what he's doing.

ANNA

Mom! Look at Beth!

(BETH *has a belt around her throat and is banging her head against the floor.*)

ANNA

(*Running to* BETH) Beth is going fast, Mom. We gotta do therapy now!

MOM

OK! OK! How do we start?

ANNA

Lie down on the couch and tell me about your childhood.

(MOM *lies on the couch.*)

MOM

What about my childhood?

ANNA

How do you feel about your parents?

MOM

They were lovely, lovely parents. Well educated, upper-middle class. They believed in God and Jesus Christ and went to church four times a week.

(BETH *is drinking Windex.* ANNA *runs to stop her.*)

MOM

My father was brilliant and successful and my mother loved me so much, so very much, so so so very very much, so so so so so so so so so so so so so so so so so very very much much much much much much much much much much—

ANNA

I know she loved you, Mom! Can't you tell me about
conflicts? Anger?

MOM

Anger?

ANNA

(Struggling with BETH) Yeah, Mom.

MOM

(Murderously) There was never any anger.

*(*BETH *is trying to strangle herself by putting a plastic bag
over her head.)*

ANNA

(Struggling with BETH) There had to be some anger.
Everyone experiences anger at some point.

MOM

(Even more murderously) NO ANGER! *(Rising off the
couch)* Not one little BIT!!

ANNA

(Even more struggling) All the psychologists agree, Mom.
You can't do therapy without talking about anger.

MOM

We were a GOOD family! WELL EDUCATED!
UPPER-MIDDLE CLASS! WE BELIEVED IN GOD
AND JESUS CHRIST. WE LOVED EACH OTHER SO
MUCH, SO VERY MUCH, SO SO SO VERY VERY
MUCH, SO SO SO SO SO SO SO SO SO—

ANNA

(Desperately struggling) I KNOW YOU LOVED EACH
OTHER!!

MOM

(Desperate) Every day after school I sat waiting by Daddy's office door. I would dress up in my prettiest pink dress and my sweetest pink bow. My hands were folded so nicely in my lap and my knees were pressed so tightly together and every day I waited and waited and waited and waited and waited and waited and waited, but Daddy never came out of his office. He never even peeped just to see what I looked like. It wasn't his fault. I guess he didn't know I was there.

(BETH *has gotten hold of the razor blades.*)

ANNA

Mom, help!

MOM

Momma said it would be different when I was married but it wasn't. An hour after the wedding vows my groom excused himself. "You don't mind do you. I've got some work to catch up on." I never saw him again. Sometimes at night I felt his rough hands fumbling with my secret parts, but did he ever turn on the light? Did he ever look at my face?

ANNA

(Struggling more with BETH) Mom, you gotta help me!

MOM

BETH! You haven't been using your Chap Stick, HAVE YOU?! You've let your lips get chapped AGAIN! Do you know what doctors do when your lips get chronically chapped? THEY CUT THEM OFF!

ANNA

(Desperately, desperately struggling) Mom!

MOM

I read about this in *Better Homes and Gardens*. They don't put you to sleep. They don't give you anything to dull the pain. They cut slowly around your mouth and if you move or scream HALF YOUR FACE GETS SLICED OFF, TOO!

(ANNA *is now trying to keep* BETH *from cutting her throat.*)

ANNA

Help me, Mom! I can't control her!

(MOM *reaches under the couch and pulls out the baseball bat.*)

MOM

Beth? Don't you have some practicing to do? Aren't you playing music for church tomorrow? *(Threatening with the bat)* I WANT YOU PRACTICING NOW!

(BETH *stops trying to kill herself and begins crawling quickly over to the music stand and instruments.*)

MOM

(Threatening with the stick) STOP! *(*BETH *stops.)* Stand up!...STAND! *(With tremendous effort,* BETH *stands.)* WALK! *(Tentatively,* BETH *takes a step, then another, then another.* MOM *follows her with the bat.* BETH *picks up a violin case.)*

MOM

NOT THE VIOLIN! THE GUITAR! *(*BETH *opens the violin case.)* I SAID THE GUITAR!!!!!!!

ANNA

Let her play the violin if she wants. We don't even have a guitar.

MOM

I SAID PLAY THE GUITAR!!!!!!!!!!!!!!!!!!!!!!!!!!!!!!!!!!!!

(BETH *looks at her mother. She starts to put the violin down.
But then suddenly she picks it up and plays it.*)

(MOM *goes wild. She grabs the violin and throws it across
the room, throws music all over, knocks over chairs, smashes
up the cake, and rips cushions off the couch, all while yelling
"PLAY THE GUITAR! PLAY THE GUITAR!"* ANNA
*follows her mother around, trying to find some way to stop
this tirade.*)

ANNA

(Crying) Mommy. Mommy.

(*Meanwhile* BETH *has crawled to the violin and now begins
playing it again.* MOM *smashes* BETH *over the head with the
bat.* BETH *screams and crawls away.* MOM *follows, hitting.*
ANNA *is screaming as well.* BETH *crawls behind the couch;*
MOM *follows. Over and over we see the bat smash down on*
BETH, *who is now hidden by the couch.*)

MOM

(In a frenzy, as she hits) Hit me back! I can't stop! Hit me
back! Hit me back! I can't stop! Hit me back! Hit me
back! Hit me back! Hit me back!

(ANNA, *who has been trying to stop her mother, finally
succeeds in yanking her down to the ground. Lying on her
back on the floor,* MOM *is still swinging.*)

MOM

Hit me back! Hit me back! Hit me back!

(ANNA *slaps her. She stops swinging.* ANNA *helps her
mother up.*)

MOM

(Weeping bitterly) I'm a terrible mother. I'm a terrible
mother. I try to be a good mother but it never works
out. I don't know what happens. It's not my fault. I
guess Momma was right. I'm wicked. I soiled my bed. I

got dirt on my white church gloves. The devil was in me, she said. Every day I can see it more and more in your face, she said. You're wicked. So very wicked, so so so very very wicked, so so so so so so so so so so—

(With ANNA's help, BETH crawls from behind the couch. She is badly beaten. Her limbs shake.)

MOM
(Sinks to her knees) Heavenly Father take my life, please? I don't deserve to live. I love my children and look what I do. Let me die so my children can stop suffering so. Take my life before I hurt another hair—

(BETH holds a razor blade out to MOM.)

MOM
(Seeing the razor blade) You want me to kill myself? You want your own mother to kill herself? *(Jumps up and starts running in circles around the room)* All right! I'll kill myself! I'll do it! If my own child wants me dead I might as well kill myself! I'll drive off a cliff and smash myself against the rocks below! (MOM *lunges for the front door.* ANNA *throws herself across the door, barring* MOM's *exit.)*

ANNA
You can't leave, Mom! Dad won't allow you out of the house!

MOM
(Suddenly calm) That's right.

(BETH collapses. ANNA *runs to her, feels her pulse.)*

ANNA
She's dying, Mom. What do we do?

MOM

We can't take her to a hospital. Your father won't let me out of the house.

ANNA

I'd take her myself but I can't lift her. I'm only ten. I know! Isn't Dad a doctor?

MOM

I can't exactly remember. It's been so long.

ANNA

We get mail delivered here to a Dr. Paul Hamlin so he must be a doctor. I'm going in there and tell him to come out.

MOM

(Terrified) You're going into his office?

ANNA

It's the only way, Mom.

MOM

But you've never even met the man. Who knows what he's like?!

ANNA

I've got to try it!

MOM

But that door hasn't been opened in 25 years! What if he's annoyed?

ANNA

We can settle all that later in family therapy. Right now we've got to think of Beth's life!

(ANNA *opens Father's Office just a crack and peeks in. Immediately she slams it shut again.*)

ANNA

Oh my God.

(Terrified, MOM *steps slowly up to the door, peeks in, slams it shut.)*

ANNA

Mom! You know what this means? It means you're free! You can leave the house! You can take Beth to the hospital!!!

MOM

No I can't dear. I keep telling you. Your father won't let me out of the house.

ANNA

Forget about Dad, Mom. We've got to save Beth!

MOM

Oh dear. We have to clean up this mess. I'm having a birthday party. *(Starts picking up as she hums* Happy Birthday.*)*

ANNA

Her pulse is fading! Mom, you gotta help me lift her! We gotta get her to the hospital!

MOM

Speak up, dear. I can't hear you. *(Continues humming)*

ANNA

You gotta help me lift her!!

MOM

I can't hear you, dear.

ANNA

(In tears) Mom! She's dying! Please help me lift her!

MOM

There must be something wrong with my ears. I can't
hear a word you're saying.

(ANNA *pulls with all her might on* BETH's *arm, trying to
drag her out of the house as—*)

MOM

(As she cleans) I can never sit down. This house is never
clean. I clean and clean but it never gets clean. I never
get to rest. There is no rest for the wicked the Bible says.
I must be so wicked. So very wicked. So so so very very
wicked. So so so so so so so so so so so so so so so—

ANNA

Mom. She's dead.

MOM

Oh no! Not Beth too! *(Collapses, weeping)*

ANNA

You could have saved her, Mom.

MOM

I loved her so much.

ANNA

You could have saved her.

MOM

So very much. So so so very very much. So so so so so—
(ANNA *stands and crosses off.*) —so so so so so so—

ANNA

(Re-entering with a suitcase) I gotta go, Mom.

MOM

So so so so so—

ANNA

I don't want to. It's just....

MOM

So so so so very very—

ANNA

(Lip quivers) Goodbye, Beth.

MOM

Very very very very—

ANNA

Goodbye, Mom.

MOM

Very very very very very—

ANNA

Goodbye.

MOM

Much much much much much much much—

(ANNA exits out the front door.)

MOM

Much much much much much. *(Suddenly cheerful)* Well.
(She stands—goes to Father's Office door) Sweetheart! It's
time to come out of your office! It's time for my
birthday party!

*(MOM picks up a chunk of cake and sets it on the table. She
sticks candles in it and lights the candles.)*

MOM

(Calling—as she lights the candles) Beth? Anna? Don't you
want to come to your mother's birthday party? Brett
Spencer Clifford? It's your mother's birthday party!
Bobbie?... Your father's coming. The whole family's

coming to my birthday party!... Jimmy? Jerry? Johnnie? Jody? Jamie? Josie? Jenny? Jannie? Joshie? Jeremy? Janie? Jerry? Joey? George?... Your father's coming out of his office any minute.... Julie? Jeffery?... Any minute...Tad? *(She look's at Father's Office door. She goes to the door. She opens the door wide. It is a brick wall with one brick missing. A man's eyes stare at her through the missing brick.* MOM *smiles at him; at last he sees her! Then his hand comes up and he places the last brick in place. Her tears flood.)* Doesn't anyone want to come to my birthday party?

LIGHTS FADE. END OF PLAY.